Cousins
by Lola M. Schaefer

Consulting Editor: Gail Saunders-Smith, Ph.D.

Consultant: Phyllis Edelbrock, First-Grade Teacher,
University Place School District, Washington

Pebble Books

an imprint of Capstone Press
Mankato, Minnesota

1

Pebble Books are published by Capstone Press
818 North Willow Street, Mankato, Minnesota 56001
http://www.capstone-press.com

Library of Congress Cataloging-in-Publication Data
Schaefer, Lola M., 1950–
    Cousins/by Lola M. Schaefer.
    p. cm.—(Families)
    Includes bibliographical references and index.
    Summary: Simple text and photographs depict cousins and what they can
do with each other and their other relatives.
    ISBN 0-7368-0254-1
    1. Cousins—Juvenile literature. [1. Cousins.] I. Title. II. Series: Schaefer,
Lola M., 1950–   Families.
HQ759.95.S33   1999
306.87—dc21   98-46134
                                                                                    CIP
                                                                                     AC

Note to Parents and Teachers

The Families series supports national social studies standards for units related to identifying family members and their roles in the family. This book describes and illustrates cousins and activities they do with each other. The photographs support emergent readers in understanding the text. The repetition of words and phrases helps emergent readers learn new words. This book also introduces emergent readers to subject-specific vocabulary words, which are defined in the Words to Know section. Emergent readers may need assistance to read some words and to use the Table of Contents, Words to Know, Read More, Internet Sites, and Index/Word List sections of the book.

Table of Contents

daughter ← mother   daughter ↔ mother

sister ← sister

cousin ← → cousin

niece → aunt

aunt ← → niece

4

Cousins are children
of aunts or uncles.

Some cousins are girls.

Some cousins are boys.

Some cousins visit
on holidays.

Some cousins visit
on vacations.

Some cousins ride bikes.

Some cousins eat treats.

17

Some cousins go sledding.

Sometimes cousins
sleep over.

Words to Know

aunt—the sister of a person's mother or father; an aunt also can be the wife of a person's uncle.

cousin—the child of a person's aunt or uncle

holiday—a special day that people celebrate

uncle—the brother of a person's mother or father; an uncle also can be the husband of a person's aunt.

vacation—a trip away from home

visit—to go see people or places away from home

Read More

Baxter, Nicola. *Families.* Chicago: Children's Press, 1996.

Laden, Nina. *My Family Tree: A Bird's-Eye View.* San Francisco: Chronicle Books, 1997.

Saunders-Smith, Gail. *Families.* People. Mankato, Minn.: Pebble Books, 1998.

Skutch, Robert. *Who's in a Family?* Berkeley, Calif.: Tricycle Press, 1995.

Internet Sites

Family.com
http://family.go.com

Family First
http://hometown.aol.com/BMValen/index.html

The Family Fun Network—Kids Room
http://www.ffn.org/kids.htm

Index/Word List

are, 5, 7, 9
aunts, 5
bikes, 15
boys, 9
children, 5
cousins, 5, 7, 9, 11, 13,
   15, 17, 19, 21
eat, 17
girls, 7

go, 19
holidays, 11
ride, 15
sledding, 19
sometimes, 21
treats, 17
uncles, 5
vacations, 13
visit, 11, 13

Word Count: 41
Early-Intervention Level: 4

Editorial Credits
Mari C. Schuh, editor; Steve Weil/Tandem Design, cover designer and illustrator;
   Kimberly Danger, photo researcher

Photo Credits
Arthur Tilley/FPG International LLC, 1, 8
David F. Clobes, 4, 20
International Stock/Scott Barrow, cover
John Terence Turner/FPG International LLC, 18
Kay Hendrich, 16
Palma Allen, 6, 12
Photo Network/Myrleen Cate, 14
Rebecca Christensen, 10

Special thanks to Joy Allison, Lori Hollenback, and Penny McCarthy, first-grade
teachers at Evergreen Primary in University Place, Washington, for reviewing the
books in the Families series.